The Mouth in the Sky

Also by Dominic Kirwan and published by Ginninderra Press
Miracles Become Monsters
Put a Smile On That Face
Where Words Go When They Die
The Holy Babble

Dominic Kirwan

The Mouth in the Sky

This book is dedicated to the loving memory of my best friend,
Andrew David Coote, 1970–2021
R.I.P.

I would like to thank my beautiful, kind-hearted mother,
Barbara, for sticking by me through what seemed to be
impossible odds, for loving me despite all my shortcomings
and my relentless mental illness. Her indomitable spirit
guided me through a hell I would not have survived alone.
Without her support, this book would not exist.

I would like to thank Bridget Kirwan
for her creative assistance with the cover.

The Mouth in the Sky
ISBN 978 1 76109 498 9
Copyright © text Dominic Kirwan 2023
Cover image: *Overdose*, an original work by Dominic Kirwan

First published 2023 by
GINNINDERRA PRESS
PO Box 3461 Port Adelaide 5015
www.ginninderrapress.com.au

Contents

Andy	9
The Flaccid Return of the People's Champion	10
A Walk in the City	13
Padding the Walls	17
Thankyou	20
Disguise in Love With You	21
The Sound of Father	24
Best	28
Diet Lemonade	33
A Toast to Her Ghost in Absentia	36
A Grotesquery of Stars	39
Products and Accessories (To Murder)	44
Pinocchio	48
Leonard Cohen Peach	51
The Tale End of the Queue	52
Just People	56
Suburban Vampire	58
Asylum Eye	59
Ghost Flesh	64
Give the Man a Hand	65
Grateful	68
Heavy Metal Cheddar	69
The Suicide Show	72
Wake Me When It's Over	75
The Trouble with Hair	77
The Unimportance of Being Earnest (Hemingway)	80
The Most Interesting Person You Know	83
The Flavour of That Time of the Month	87
The Way Out	89
Anti-hero Quest	90

A Place Where Nothingness is No Longer a Word	93
For Angels There to See	95
Masks	99
Tear-shaped Swastika	100
The Severing of Strings	103
The Imaginary Play	106
Upon Reflection	110
Fat from Dreams	112
Voices	114

'I am a cage, in search of a bird.'
Franz Kafka

Andy

The voices are silent now.
They cannot hurt you any more.
But I can still love you,
My sweet, wonderful friend
And I always will.

The Flaccid Return of the People's Champion

The road home is paved with appropriate clichés
You take your demons with you
Just to cast them out
Just to start all over again
In the same place that ruined you

Have I written this all before?
Have I snorted these same lines a million times?

I'm scratching at the abdomen of a deadly spider
As if it were a bemused pet
Headphones and silence blaring loud
An answering
A calling
A ringing
Fingers in my ears
The never-ending echoes of new neighbours
The strangled cries of a panicked ambulance
Walks in a city where my nature left me
Loneliness and independence
Startled procedures and simpleton suicides
Stepped on syringes, bleeding black river milk
Benign cancers blossoming into flowers
with unpronounceable names

The road home is paved with patented inventions
Old bed
Old fan
Old darkness
Old haunt
New me
Different me
I don't know where else I can belong

Wondering about shallow used-to-bees
The buzzing
The stinging
The swarming
Unfamiliar comfort and dishes clattering in an old sink

I pray to a god I don't believe in
I pray to a god who doesn't believe in me
I pray to psychosocial experiments gone awry
I pray to mental institutions filled with actors
I pray to a fiend
I pray to public transport and a fraying blue mask
I pray to fluorescent, bleached supermarket faces in hiding
I pray to the pulsating, forlorn city
I pray to the medication that lobotomises me
I pray to serpentine bone trains and panic stations
I pray to covid, so the virus won't catch a case of me
I pray to the Uber

I pray to clumsy laughter and an absentee wit
I pray to Death Metal's twitching Carcass
I pray to surround sound speakers and encroaching head shrinkers
I pray to life, in all its unmitigated horror
I pray to the friends I have left

Every misstep is incalculable
Every numb, brain rattling breath a lesson
Every drug addled, whimpering limp is a falsity

The camera lens expands for the Masters
And I step back
and back and back and back
Caught, like the most violent karma,
In the spying eye of an unforgiving goldfish

Roar meat
Stick a fork in my head
I'm yodelling, churning the other cheek like rotisserie
Pussy-walk modelling for team Jesus
Baste me
Taste me
Bend me over the green fire
Serve me up to the congregation
I am done

A Walk in the City

I step outside the front door
As if it were a portal loo to a septic world
FearOfStrangers Street greets me like an old fiend
All traffic fire, sky sewerage and disconcerting echo
Another left and SnarlOrYou'llSurelyPerish Street unravels
Stretching out like unpainted canvass
beneath blistered soles

I cross the road to avoid roadworks
The path is not wide enough for anything but single file
Bones move inside loose fitting flesh and
disconnected muscle tissue and sinew

Will I fall over if someone touches me?
Will my bones tumble out of my holes and form a tableau?
Will they scatter and crumble, carried forever away by the wind?
leaving jellied, pet food meat
and a deserted brain,
finally freed of the jar that pickled it
With nothing left but vinegared reminiscences
to hold it in

Will it too roll away?
A pretentious, spidery blob
scurrying between cracks in concrete
chasing mindless, murderous cars and trucks
nipping at the rubber ankles of lumbering buses,
pregnant with masked mannequins

A lady with hips as wide as the pathway
wearing stretched close to snapping jeans
and carrying two bags of groceries
turns and crosses the road to avoid an inevitable collision
this happens again and again

My mind is a revolving door
A grubby paperback to be burnt before reading
There is a skittish hand grenade
Nervously rattling behind my eyes

A rail thin reptile with a bleached mullet
and dark wraparound sunglasses slithers by,
dragging on a cigarette, wet from his slavering
There is a gust of turgid wind
His scales suddenly scatter the air like grey confetti
Exposing him
They billow into a plume of disturbed leaves
I breathe in, inhaling sharply
there is something beneath
there is always something beneath

Meth by Lauriel

I pass a beautiful Indian woman
wearing blood red lipstick and analyse-me slacks
She smiles at me kindly
She knows something I do not
She reminds me of my former psychiatrist
I wonder if, like me, she is taking mental notes

My wavering gait is tenuous
I cannot walk in a straight-line
People notice this from a distance and,
as they approach,
they consider an alternative pathway

Another left through several crosswalk lights
with elbow buttons, knee buttons, personality buttons
and 'knows better but presses it anyway' buttons
that magically manipulate angry red men
into vain green ones

I begin the process of run experiments
They last 40 to 50 sometimes 100 metres at a time
The Olympics are calling
I am shattering records in slow motion
Running as fast as able-bodied people walk
I pass no one
I am no one
Epileptic seizures manifest
I wrestle to be free of an invisible straitjacket
There are wet tampons in my eyes
There is an information leak in my heart
Bones threaten to splinter, crumble into nose powder
This is just another experiment

I spy a baby's pacifier on the ground in the grass
A wee yellow dummy reflecting the light of the sun
A recently slobbered on talisman
Nearby is an empty, abandoned stroller
Was a baby mugged here?
This is all that remains of the crime
Everywhere about me there are clues
Mmmmmm Covid…
I can almost smell you

Delta Strain by Chanel

I take a final left onto FearOfStrangers Street
Devoid of easily catalogued courage
I awkwardly spasm up the final hill
Under the overpass that leads me home
Although, there is no tangible finish line that I can see
Just more pathways, spiralling from the mouth in the sky
Reaching out forever in the darkness,
gasping for unsullied air

There is no convenient ending
for such poetry
Just hope

Padding the Walls

What would happen
If you got exactly what you always wanted?
Would you smile?
Would you rise into the sky like an angel?
Would you rain down love
on all those that cried out for it?
Or would you roll over in bed
Like a slab of flyblown meat
And drift off back to sleep?

You padded the walls of your universe
All on your own
And now you're crying out for love?
Once someone gets invited inside
They cannot wait to leave

It feels like
He hated you
Before you even escaped the womb
And still, to this day
You see yourself through his eyes

Perhaps a lonely heart
Is what you deserve
Some people are bleeding
Long before the razor
Is applied to the vein

Who started the war in your mind?
Is it winnable?
No one ever won a war
Not ever
They just got permission from history
To write about it
As if by their very nature
Cruelty and compassion are interlinked
By ink

There must be a way out of this loop
But you cannot find it

People say –
Love yourself a little more
Be kind to yourself
Forgive yourself

But you just can't do it

What would it be like
If you got exactly what you always wanted?

Perhaps you already have it

You write about a battle
That cannot be won
You write about that battle
As if you have perished a thousand times

The Monster sits at your desk
Punching your keys
Punching your clock
Rewriting your feelings
Rewriting your losses
Rewriting your faces
Rewriting your heart, your mind and
Your rotting paper soul
Your intentions have been rewritten over and
Over and over and over
So many times, now
Surely
All of this will come to an end

For who is it, my friend,
Who is holding the pen?

Thankyou

It's so sad
The way she's sees him now
Perpetual déjà vu, blue eyes retreating
Squinting in the twilight, praying
for a secret to keep him safe from himself
There's not much left for her to love
but she loves him anyway

He's leaving one home for another

By the time he realised,
it was all too late
He's leaving his best friend behind

Don't be a stranger, Son
Come back another day, she says
But the way home is disappearing,
the road between hearts, fading from view
He can see it closing, like his mind
One synaptic snap back at a time
A sullen cul-de-sac ending

He's leaving one home for another

My mind is gone, he says
and I'm scared of everything and everyone but you

It's what's in here that matters most, she replies
and with subtle emphasis
she lightly taps her beating chest

Disguise in Love With You

I love you like arsenic
sweating from the rigid pistil
of an exquisite flower
I love you like a slavering tongue
lapping at poisoned petals
I love you like Tuesday
simply because it's not Wednesday
I love you for no other reason
than to hunt you down
and haunt your bones

I love you when you investigate the mirror with disgust
I love you when you lie to yourself to feel better
I love you when you make-believe that you are free
I love you when you spank the jabbering monkey
I love you when you are someone else more lovable
I love you when you are me

I love you like nervous black tar,
bubbling like lava in wheezing lungs
I love you like the sequel to a movie
that sucked the first-time around
I love you like tomorrow's doomed diet
and yesterday's existential pizza
I love you like an undiscovered brain tumour,
waiting excitedly to be found

I love you when you choke on the barrel
and wounded crocodile tears fill your eyes
I love you when you cum
and go as if people care
I love you like scene-of-the-crime tyre tracks
on telling brown underwear

I love you like a trigger warning worth squeezing
I love you like a boy band,
all killed in a mysterious inferno
I love you like suicide and green fire and lollipop leukaemia
I love you like a gummy vampire
searching the internet for hen's teeth
I love you like a rabid dog
gnawing on a medicated god

I love you when you're the only drunk in the room
and it's still turning
I love you when you're dressed-to-ill
and spiralling downtown
I love you when you're a far-fetched blur in slow motion
I love you when you crack sick jokes at funerals
and you can't understand why nobody is laughing

I love you,
even when you're raping rainbows
I love you,
even when you're defiling the perfect sunset

I love you despite the hell in your heart
I love you despite the war in your mind

Ah, such delusional grandeur for one so peculiarly small!
Such lewd deception and irreconcilable folly
Oh, I do so love it when you tell the truth…

I don't love you.

The Sound of Father

The sound of beer bottles exploding
Often woke the Boy late at night
There was a small metal shed
Outside the window of his bedroom
Its interior was lined with shelves of home-brewed beer
Each bottle contained a single plump prune
Forced down every bottle neck
Like another hard to swallow lesson
It was Father's secret recipe
It was a dangerous and unpredictable combination

The sound of Father

If the explosion of brown glass
Didn't kill him when he was in the shed
Fetching beers for Father
Then the random blasts of beer bottles suiciding
Would startle the Boy
Interrupting his dreams
Like the drunken blow
Of a wildly swung sledgehammer
It was often a chain reaction
Every exploding bottle had the potential
To destroy the ones surrounding it

The thirst of Father

Generally, bottles explode due to pressure
Caused by over-carbonation
If a beer is bottled before fermentation is complete
Or if a beer is bottle-conditioned
There is fermentation happening in the bottle
The resulting carbon dioxide
Can build up enough
To break glass
To explode

The failed science of Father

The Boy was tasked with sweeping up the detritus
Of these random explosions
During the day
The concrete floor of the shed
Remained sticky and brown grey in texture
When the doors were open
The invading sunshine caused the concrete to glisten
Like morning light
Caught in Father's bloodshot eyes
There was no time for mopping up the ooze
Sweeping was quicker
There was no lingering in the shed

The unpredictability of Father

Before Father's home-brewing phase
The chickens in the open yard
Secretly laid their eggs in the shed
Hoarding them, squatting on them in a dark corner
A pathological maternal instinct
Wired into each bird's brain
Buried, like the potential to please Mother
Under layers of well-intentioned feathers and shit
Once Father's beer bottles moved into their nesting place
The explosions started
And the chickens laid their eggs elsewhere
The dangerous blasts necessitated closure
Most of the time
The doors to the shed remained closed and bolted

The will of Father

Sometimes the Boy would imagine
What it would be like
To enter the shed at night
And wedge the metal doors shut behind him
To wait in the darkness
The stench of stale beer invading his delirium
The potential for another mass explosion
That would change everything

The love of Father

A fatal misstep in a claustrophobic minefield
The fatal kiss of a thousand mad bees
Glass shards piercing his flesh
Holding his breath
Walking on last summer's eggshells
Crunching shards of broken glass
Beneath his feet
Lashings of blood and beer
Painting the walls of the Boy's terrified mind
The staggered hiccupping of his pulse
Segueing into numb detonations of stillness

The absence of Father

Fearful shadows trapped in a small metal shed
That may as well have been a mind
That may as well have been Asylum
Echoes of a Boy's stifled laughter
Silenced forever

The lasting memory of Father

Best

He was the best
There was no doubt about it
Everyone thought so
His very being
Was lathered in fictional swathes
Of bestness.

Although, why he dwelt in fear
Of their pointed and perilous mockery
Was still a mystery
That evaded him.

The green room in his mind
Was furnished regally
There was an unoccupied bar
Stocked with half empty whisky bottles
Covered in dust and dead skin
Which, as everybody knows
Is the same damn thing.

Oh, and a ping pong table
For batting the balls
For cupping the sprightly white
Plastic balls
Of absolute best-ness.

There was a revolving door
In the back of his head
It was manned by underpaid security
Two borderline personality disorder schmucks
High on steroids and calculated brawn
And several ungiven, zero-fucks.

The bouncers were just happy
To work the doorway
They hoped for a promotion
And a significant pay upgrade
They were like everyone else, yes
Hoping, as one does
For the very best.

Those who braved the green room
Had leprechaun logic
And pots of Irish gold in mind
Yet there were no ravished rainbows
On the horizon
No prisons of prism
To be seen
They left empty-headed
And empty-handed
Feeling better, greener
Yet so much worse
Than ever before.

His entire life
Had been a contextualised metaphor
For first place
For the betterment of all that it means
To be the best
But what good would that do him now?

Those who came up short
In his estimation
Noted he was so much taller
And they stared longingly up at him
Seeking guidance
Hoping to be better, the best.

They inhaled the dandruff
That rained down upon his giant shoulders
They stood there, pontificating
As if the dandruff were magical halo snow
Or primo Columbian cocaine.

Silver tongue in cheek
He forbade last place
Second or third would not suffice
The newspaper headlines
Dubbed him the only thing
Worth watching
In an unwatchable, amateur
Passionless play
Where he ruled the land
As a one-eyed king.

'A troubled rat,' they labelled him:
'Drowning, in a swirling morass
Of existential faeces.'

On the press tour
On a rare visit to a casino
Sitting at the high rollers table
Engaged in a game of hypothetical poker
He upped his bet, to 'all in'
He pushed his soul into the centre
Of the felt and feeling-less green

Yet, moments later
In a crisis of confidence
And most inexplicably
He folded his hand

The sudden move
Was met with chagrin sneers
From the other gamblers
Who knew best
When they could beat it
Who knew much better
Than to fold
On a royal lavatory flush

He pissed his last chance away
He gambled away his humanity
In life, as in death
There is no second prize.

Outside the courtroom casino
He devoured a sweaty bag
Of magical mushrooms
And proceeded to un-seize the day.

When asked to comment
On his unusual predicament
He merely winked slyly
And again, folded on his entire hand.

With a dejected groan
He limped off into the unforgiving night
'You guys are the worst,' he was heard to say
As he hobbled away
His voice trailing off
In defeated waves of bested echo.

'It was all for the best,' everyone who had survived him said.
For that was the part they could all agree on.

In a spectacularly vulgar display
Of poetic injustice
He had finally surrendered his pen
He was never heard from
Or seen,
Ever again.

Diet Lemonade

'There is no writing your way out of this one,'
Said the Judge

'I hereby sentence you
To three consecutive life sentences
Without the possibility of rewrites
Or access
To any grammatically driven spellcheck program
No matter how literary
Or necessary to your story
They may be.'

'These conjoined sentences may seem harsh,'
Continued the Judge
Wiping the moisture from his furrowed brow
'But they are necessary,
For I aim to make an example of you
So that other smutty fiction peddlers
Might learn something from your depraved
Misguided pathos
And shun the dangerous allure
Of a life spent tapping keys
And punching happy people…
And instead –
Do something with their lives!'
The Judge continued, righteously huffing
Now on a ham roll

'Like work in retail as a store detective
In the fat fuck section
And help put an end to overweight shoplifting,'
The Judge blabbered on and on,
He was now clearly aroused
Tightly gripping his gavel with one hand
He secretly, sensuously
Stroked the bulging wrath
Of his misshapen balls
With the other

'Or join a respectable theatre company,'
The Judge continued
'And take all of that bad direction
All those opening night jitters
All those snarky reviews
That define every line of dialogue
Spoken or written
As lemons
And instead, skip the compulsory addition
Of sweetness
And turn those goddamn lemons
Ladies and Gentlemen
Into Diet Lemonade!'

The Judge was well pleased with his inspired spieling
He was close to climaxing

Yet before he could continue
The Writer pulled out a gun
He waved it menacingly at the Judge and the Jury
Smiled like he'd just figured out a great ending
For the unfolding story
Turned the weapon on himself
And blew his brains out

Covered in blood, gore
Cerebral soup and confettied bone
The members of the courtroom lapsed
Into an inconvenient silence
But soon they began to rise to their feet
One by one by one, until finally...
They erupted in rapturous applause

A Toast to Her Ghost in Absentia

She entered my line of vision
Like a portrait of pilfered breath
She liberated the air from my lungs
She held up a mirror
And with a series of simple, exasperated glances
She laid bare my yearning
For everything
For nothing
For something better than this
She tore the fan from my ceiling
While it was steadily revolting
And I knew
Nothing would ever be the same

She stretched me like a canvass
Over an artist's rendering
Of Dorian Gray's blackened liver

Feigning waves of grandiosity
And out of sight of the Church
I canonised her
Dubbing her Saint and salacious star
I uncoiled for her God
Hissy fitting like a fruitarian Serpent

I laid it on thick, I did
My charm swiftly turned to chunder
I offered her a mouthful of madness
A teaspoon of blubbering whale harpooned
A toast to her ghost in absentia
She declined
And I woefully drowned in my folly

I throttled the room
A drunken jackhammer
Unaware of my own egotisms
Running my drooling gob
Marathoning my mouth
As if trapped in a loop
In a farcical infomercial
For fitness equipment
For un-fun runs
And the tolling of dumb bells

Belching into the empty canyon
Of my own making
I drowned in waves of arrogant echo

But then something changed
Something unseen and imperceptible
The music lifted
She smiled kindly and rose to her feet
And she began to dance…

Swaying like an exotic creature
Rhythmic, Seismic, Sensual
Hypnotic textures and immersive gestures
Of lithe flow and grace
Of miracle crystal chaste and subliminal taste
A haunting ballet for fractured minds
And the cataclysmic crescendo
Of dreamers and true believers
Rising up
Ready, finally, to be devoured
By the mysterious mouth in the sky

I don't know anything any more
Perhaps I never did
All I know is that she danced
And it was one of the most beautiful things
I ever saw

A Grotesquery of Stars

1.

On his way to the circus of the slain
The Cretin crept like a creep
As creeps are wont to do
He staggered drunk through a garden labyrinth
Of immaculately trimmed hedges
And mentally unstable hedged bets.

The stars guided him
On through the maze
Monitoring his movements like radar
Yet failing to bleep out the vulgarities
That fled from his inebriated maw
Like dejected rats
Escaping a burning black lodge.

The hyper real moon.
The black sun.
A grotesquery of stars.
United
Smearing pixels of lard
Across the Cretin's heart
Fattening his resolve.

The Circus Master chanced upon the Cretin
Cowering in the garden, lost
And he snatched him up
He led him into the main-event tent
Guiding him via a tightening noose
That was more of a leash
For a wounded, beaten dog
Than a deliberate attempt at writing
A foregone conclusion.

The Cretin brayed and wept, spent of elegance.

'Why does it always have to end this way?' he thought.

The Circus Master squeezed the trigger
A warning shot without a trigger warning
That ploughed through flesh nonetheless
He smirked snarkily: a charming reptile.
He bowed regally, flexing his scales as he did so.

Canned laughter rattled within the Cretin's emptied pâte
He scooped up handfuls of his own brains from the flaw
And eagerly, hungrily, he ate them
Stuffing his face with the former contents
Of his own mind.

(Cue imaginary audience salivating.)

At intermission
An aroused Clown grabbed at his ankles
And took last place in stride
'No funny business. Move along now,' said the Circus Master
'There is nothing to love here.'

(Cue the beatings of canned masturbation.)

'Hear, hear,' cried the Cretin, hoping to be heard
As he too dropped his draws
Mimicking the scene-stealing clown
He nervously jiggled his exposed behind
For the rolling cameras.

(Cue canned vomiting.)

The invisible audience leapt from their seats
And descended upon the Cretin as one.

'Wait your turn! Wait your turn!' the Circus Master chided.
'There is more than enough flesh here to feed everyone.'
'Take only what you need,' he said solemnly
Secretly hoping that Jesus might be listening in.

The Cretin deflated
Punctured by defeat
Pummelled by loquacious scenesters
And Circus goers
Eager to apply fanciful, poetic hammerings
To the heart-cracked Cretin
As if gutting a gasping fish
That had grown allergic
To the indecipherable ways of the river.

2.

'You just can't make this shit up,' thought the Author.
'Oh, yes you fuckin' can!' replied the Reader.
As if she could read minds
As if she could read at all

3.

'This is not sexual rejection,' said the Reality Surgeon
Speaking shakily on behalf of the Cretin
He gripped a scalpel and applied its sharp edge
To the page, to the poem
To the empty stage, to the Circus cage
To an exposed vein
'Neither is this romantic abandonment,' he continued
No longer certain who or what to cut next
'Yet it is fanciful in all ways except these…'

His voice suddenly clouded over
Smeared in an oily melody
He spoke in weary tones of reminiscence and loss:

'This is the rejection of friend.'
'This is the rejection of human.'
'This is the rejection of heart.'
'This is the rejection of man.'

4.

The self-proclaimed experts
Unwrote the ending
The snarky mind feeders of emotion and fiction
Unwrote the feeling
And the querulous Quacks of the apocalypse of imperception
Wrote nothing worth rewriting.

And when it was all over
The Cretin fell to his knees
And bawled like an abandoned god.

(Cue titillated audience snickering.)

The shark cage of unreality went suddenly, violently red
Spewing plumes of blood into the eyes of the unbelievers
The screen went beautifully and inevitably blank
The delicate light retreating as if from life itself.

The last flame ceased to dance
There was nothing left
Just the smoky wisps of a snuffed-out candle.

Products and Accessories (To Murder)

It's all about selling yourself
The real you, he doesn't matter
You are a product
So, get used to it
None of your layers or intentions are important
You are not an onion
You are an option
For you
There is only the pleasure
Of being sold

Your heart was surgically removed
From your chest
While you brazenly slept
It was on a Monday or a Tuesday or a…
Yesterday, on an *any-other-day*
And it still doesn't matter

Your heart skipped town
It is stapled to a dart board
In a smoky bar
Some deeply disturbing dive
Stinking of beer and bar-coded tabs
Bowls overflowing with urinal cake nuts
Squatting on plastic tablecloths
They remain alone and untouched
Much like you
Dreaming only
Of being mercifully devoured

All the patrons
Are tampon-tested vampires
And they're serving up stakes
Garnished
With cloves of past-tense garlic

Everyone here is a product of the times
Everyone here has murder on their mind
Everyone here is drunk on someone else's blood
Everyone here is depraved
Everyone here is a fake
Just like you

The bottom line,
Will always be a diminishing number
You are counting backwards
Down to zero
You are afraid
Of what the questions might be
You have no prepared answers

You have sold
Your version of reality
To other products
Pretending
To be people
And you Couldn't
Shouldn't and Wouldn't
Have it any other way

You are literally heartless
Empty chested and market tested
Nothing beneath the surface
Is articulable
Nothing about you is tangible
Your heart is sweet, discreet
Product meat
Marketing yourself to yourself
Has proven improbable
Yet up for sale, you remain

You remember a time
When love mattered
You remember
Lying in bed and holding her
Now, it's all about ghosts
And under-proof spirits
Sleeping alone on ill fitted sheets
And ruing the day
You converted to Loner-ism
And became a product
Of your own sorrowful design

There is no doubt about it
Inbuilt obsolescence
Is a motherfucker
And you were born to break down

So, smile
What's on the inside
No longer matters

Perhaps it is time
To turn yourself in
And finally admit to everything
That you have never done

Pinocchio

I wanna slit my throat and blame Jesus
I wanna take acid and talk to God
I wanna write a prequel
To the Bible
And call it
The Inconsequential Pity Fuck
Of Friar Nip and Tuck

Robin Hood was a dick
Maid Marion was always my heroin
And I am now in the throes
Of existential withdrawal

In my experience
The love of a woman makes you a better man
I am a bumper sticker
A wise crack from an uncommitted stalker
But my wisdom cannot be denied

I am a Lego Lobo
And there is nothing left for you to do
But to deconstruct me
And build a war out of my pieces
For me
To be
The plastic building blocks
In a twisted child's hands

Please God
Mould me into something forgiveable
Please Lucifer
Saint me and call me Father
For I am your bored game

I am ahead
In the polls in my head
I am Joan of Arc's rebellious laughter
Turn my insides upside down
Set me on unsellable fire

The tides shall swell and change
The sea sprawl will consume me
Buried up to my neck in slow sand

Forge a castle from my dead expression
Place death pennies over my eyes
Leave me to impress the tourists and naysayers
Leave me alone
Forever
As if there was anything briefer
As if there were nothing more temporary
Than a rogue army of barking barnacles
On the wooden soul, the cracked hull
Of a salty dog's shrinking ship

When one is self-unemployed
There is nothing more aromatic than the stench
Of unsmellable love

This beach, this ocean bitch,
This *Oh! Scene*
She is all around me
Still, I am just another Soldier
Longer, harder, colder, older, bolder
Than I have *never* been

I want to be a real boy
But I am an imaginary man

My growing knows
Is an unhappy gun
And I am triggered
Bullets and barrel rolled
In hidden chambers
Pressed against this holy temple
In Geppetto's shaking hands

Leonard Cohen Peach

And when the bombs fall
I will be in the periphery of your perfume
And when the apocalypse comes
I will be circling your heart
Walking like a dithering Jesus
Head held high, eyes clear,
Mud descending into chasms of belief

And as the earth opens her maw
To swallow us
I will catch you
Smother your sweet, goose pimpled flesh
In rogue kisses
Taste you like sweat,
Beading on bristling peach skin
Our shadows riveted by bitten nails
To the T-shaped tree
In the corner of your mind's eye

And when the bombs fall
So too shall we

The Tale End of the Queue

Another day
Another broken promise
Another apology
Rinse and repeat ad nauseam

But I need you…

Priorities reflected in imperfection
My unfinished tome is uncertain salvation
My dream shakes like heartbroken hands
Time itself is stalking me, always
Tick-tocking
Tick-tocking
The clock's hands
Beat down upon my cognisance
Like clenched fists that mean to bruise

The last full stop is coming
The semicolons are repeating
Angry commas gather at the edge of the ledge
Like carcinomic illiteracy
Ready to pounce on me

I am not ready for the ending
But still,
It is whispering for me to let it in
From the other side

Another day
Another broken promise
Sorry
Sorry
Sorry
And tomorrow and tomorrow and…

But I need you…

NIGHTMARE:

A mad butcher with bullet holes for eyes
Leers at me
I smile back, in frosty torment
Wondering how I got locked in this cold room
Wondering how I got locked into this contract
If only I had known

Black ink trickles from the corners of his mouth
His eyes, nose and ears are leaking
He swings his acts
I must not react
Lest I be chopped into itty-bitty pieces
And fed to the rats

How do I write myself out of this place?

AWAKE and:

I am still at the tale end of the queue
The hands of the clock are moving faster
The pause button is getting a righteous rogering
It's all dodge, shift and jive

Just breathe
Hold it in
And then exhale
Soon, the tick-tocking in your mind
This dull, peacockery panic
Will fade away

Cos you are overreacting, and you know it…

I will not crack
I will not complain
My feelings must remain invisible
One is not permitted to cry out in anguish
From the tale end of the queue

But I need you…

WARNING:

Priorities have been rearranged
You have needlessly upset the authorities
With your drama
Your true feelings are unnecessary
And so, it seems
Are you

We will get to it eventually
We will wipe your arse accordingly
We will roll your words in glitter
And correct you

When?

Tomorrow.

Just People

They're just people
Just keep saying it
They're just people
Just keep telling yourself that
And it will all be okay
They're just people
Only they aren't… Are they?
They're more than that

They're just people
You don't care what they think
They're just people
It shouldn't matter
But it does… Doesn't it?
It eats you up inside

They're just people
They live inside your head
They're just people
There are plenty more dolphins
In the tuna safe sea
So swim deep
Be captured
Be caught
Castaway

Time to move on
But you can't
But you won't
But you have no choice…so,
Let go
Let it go
Let them go

They're just people
Until they go away

The truth is a motherfucker

Suburban Vampire

The crack in an oily dinner plate moon
Separating righteous anguish
From indignation
Madness from mayonnaise

A knife
Tearing tiny holes in the sky
Creating stars
Pissing holy light
Watching from the blinding eye
Of a black storm

The mirror
Shattering into a billion fragments
Of the one mind
Reflecting chaos
Seeping into the teeth of lunatics
As they gnash and snarl
Tearing the flesh from realities' throat
Like a scythe through an insect's wing

The vampire
Mumbling obscenities
From the armpit of despair
Prodding the food on his plate with a blunt knife
To see if it is still alive enough to torture
To see if he can still see himself

Asylum Eye

They're paying the crazies
Less than minimum rage
To be silent, sedated
Humiliated
By welfare documentarians
Peddling self-help and help yourself
Pharmaceutical fart fiction

It's a conspiracy theory
For theoretical conspiracists
High on truth theorems
Their minds vandalised
By therapeutic remedies
For the zombies of tomorrow
And generation X, Y and Zed

Even if they could work
Their humanity would be subsidised
Their safety net, taken away
Full price for reality chips and
Prescriptionality scripts
Just to turn the volume switch down
From eleven to one
To mute the blabberings
Of very un-rock 'n' roll
Unreality lashings

What brand of band aid will it take?
To dilute voices, visions
To murder, with due conscience
The half-realised delusions
The whims of a living hell
And all of its *isms*
For those who would take their own lives
Without understanding or compassion
Or someone to listen
To the voices only they can hear
In a split-mind second

The imaginative minority
Drugged with propaganda pills
Necessarily popped
Like deflating
Sweetened life savers
To make way for normalcy
In raging psychotropic oceans
Typhoons unleashed
To clear a path within

You cannot cure crazy
You can gag it
You can ignore it
You can even hold someone down
And jab a needle in their arse
Once a month
With the law upon your side
You can marginalise it
With – *'You orter be indoctrinated'*
Slippery-fisted
Margarine product displacements
And oily pharmaceutical grins
Saturating fat pats on the back
And self-flagellating congratulations
For a fuck-it-all-to-hell
Job half-well done

The Consumer's that hunger
For irredeemable sanity tokens
Line up like hypnotised cattle
Skittish hooves, grinding
Into the beer-soaked carpet
Of the parlour slaughterhouse pub

Cashing souls in on pension day
For another mind-numbing
Slow-motion ride
On the rodeo clown pokies
Just to keep boredom
Bravado
And those unpaid, electro-shock
Smartphone pill bills
At bay

You cannot cure crazy
Yet you can humiliate it
Degrade and demote it
Dehumanise
Sanitise
Rape it from within
Steal from it all dignity
Pacify its victims
With the most amoral intentions

So, top 'em up
The psychotropic drug vending machines
Blow goodbye kisses
At unmedicated strangers
Applaud the lurid smugglers
Of god sweating dollar signs
Illuminated in diseased rats' eyes

You cannot silence
The expanding populace
That defines your sane rationale
You cannot hospitalise them all
You're running out of beds
There are only so many straightjackets
That will fit
Those that shit, froth and thrash
In solitary re-definement
Of whoever the fuck they are supposed to be
Banging their bleeding heads
Into the unpadded walls
You have built around them

Say hello to the rapture
And don't forget to pop your pills
You will need them
For a storm is on its way
It is all coming down
And not a moment too soon
These worlds kept so long apart
Are destined to collide

Ghost Flesh

She is the twinkle
In the eye of a dying man
Smiling as he wretches in the gutter
Grasping at the stars with stumps
Where his hands once held her
Reaching out at the broken pieces of himself
As they rise like fragments
Of ashen angels
Burnt to cinders
By the fire in her fingers

Longing for breath as the world stops turning
And all the air is sucked
From God's lungs
Promising love
Where there is only a hole
That once held a heart

Bereft of all but the hope
That there is something perfect
On the other side

The pieces have nowhere else to go
Up
Up they drift
One day they too will be amongst the stars
And the man will return
A relic of ghost flesh
Wandering aimlessly across a barren earth
In search of her

Give the Man a Hand

I got laid last night
I was completely alone
I just got lucky I guess

I was a cross-eyed tiger
Burning brightly in the darkness
I wore a wet Freudian raincoat, guilt free
I was a three-legged sex panther
In a bedroom bordello
Twerking 'tween the jungle sheets
I suspect it was a pity fuck
But still,
Just go,
Just go,
Go Me!

I cannot help it if I'm sexy
I cannot help it
If my kisses taste like the hot mulberry nectar
Of the never-never
And my sweaty palms
Weep deep stigmata tears

My saliva is the surest cure
For cancer
One swab, one sloppy kiss
And you will live forever

I am languishing
In the existential lip gloss of suffering
I am lubed up for the Oscars ceremony
Completely unprepared
For every eventuality

I have memorised my unacceptance speech
The remotest control
Is only a hop, a step and a fat screen away
I am pressing television buttons
Like an ambitious B-movie extra
In a celebrity elevator
And you can bet your pension
I will visit every flaw

The cracks in the mirror are spreading
The engine in my heart is roaring
The imaginary limousine is waiting

I got laid last night
It was magical, in a Star Snores
Ham Solo kind of way
Now my right hand won't answer my calls
And my left hand is bitter about it

I am talking to an answering machine
That won't answer any of my questions

You know
That maddening busy tone
That mobile *plan-for-something-better* phone
That you fished out of the toilet
Right before the final flush
That would have changed everything
Right before it could reach the sea
I am Home Alone
I am in the *Macaulay Culkin* zone
Go me!

I got laid last night
I was completely alone
I just got lucky I guess

It was probably a pity fuck
I woke up to a bloody stump
My right hand left me early in the morning
While I was drooling, snoring
Whatever happened to gallantry?
It's probably halfway to Hollywood already
To fulfil its wildest wet dreams
In a distant hand's free galaxy
Somewhere far, far away… From me

Grateful

the times they are achangin'
robert zimmerman sang
in distant yesterday, nasal blues
the rhymes are now
all claptrap 'n' papillon (w)rapped
the words are now
written by fighters unlike you

be grateful for what you have

the wind chills
all holy bones
the time is filled
with regrets
and panic planet anguish
with prescriptions
and unknown knowledge
with knowing only nows
and grace and impatience
with language and learnt languish
in a future world untold

Heavy Metal Cheddar

The Fiend heaved the boulder above his head
He smiled down into the tearful eyes of the Angel
As it cowered on its knees before him
With an aroused grunt, he let go
And the rock came crashing down
Upon the Angel's skull

The Seraph crumbled to the ground
A pool of red rapidly spread out
From beneath its demolished cranium
Like an inconvenient halo

The Angel's wings
Receded into its shoulder blades
Convulsing in the death throes
As the malaise of its consciousness
Went suddenly blank

The valley shimmered with death
Littered with mountains of burning Angel flesh
And the ghostly markings
Of barren womb-stones

Wisps of flyblown soul-meat
Reverberated in waves of precious echo
Slurped into the Fiend's voracious nostrils
Holy light pissing into his chest cage
Imprisoned forever in tumorous lungs

Bone fragments and nerve endings
Swam in the expanding sea of blood
They wept like illiterate foetuses
Plucked from the depths
Of tepid, last-supper soup
As if torn from a screaming womb

'Look lovingly upon my works, Father…'
Said the Fiend

He regarded the sky
'For I am the New Light,' he said
And then gestured regally
At the lifeless creature at his feet

The Fiend surveyed his surroundings
A wreckage of divine carnage
The bloody, charred feathers
Of a thousand dead angels
Wafted upwards
Towards the mad mouth
That had suddenly appeared
In the defeated, swarthy sky above him

Yet soon, the Fiend began to sob and tremble…

He reached into the wet, bloodied pockets
Of his studded leather pants
And nervously rummaged around
Until he found what he was looking for

The Fiend retrieved a half empty packet
Of Marlboro cigarettes
And a shiny Zippo
He shakily lit a durry
With his nail-bitten, nicotine-stained fingers
And took a long, well-deserved drag

Through a torrent of crazed tears
And plumes of noxious cigarette smoke
He whispered something
Finally
Just loud enough
So that his Father could hear still him –

'For I am your only Son
And I destroy all of this for you…'

The Suicide Show

Roll up! Roll up!
On me from behind
You're in a wheelchair
And I'm practising that funny walk
You used to do

The more plasma
The harder the laughter
My slit throat
Is a smile
I would dance for you
But I'm up to my neck in blood
I'm the opening act
For someone infamous
Who used to be me

There is nothing more fun than death
When the Suicide Show
Is the scheduled entertainment
Everybody goes home
With a smile on their dial
With a moist mind
Filled with entertaining memories
To tell friends and alluring strangers
At hip, underground drug parties
As if they were personal anecdotes
Worth embellishing
Yes, stories of honour, horror and pageantry
That were never theirs to tell

It's times like these
That I long for an audience
And a captivating reason to die
It's in moments such as these
That a slow, deep kiss
Would persuade me otherwise
Is that bile I can taste?
Or is it the non-profit
Of my literary vomit?

Either way
I am here to write your face away

I can't make-believe
When I am having difficulty breathing
When I am leisurely disappearing
From this pay per view asylum
Lurking in the backstages
Stalked by a self-absorbed disease
Fighting off a contagious extravaganza strain
That white coat reptiles
Designed in a secret laboratory
Specifically, just for me

I am well intentioned
I am not of this world
I am possessed
Of a semi-erect intellect
And the well-mannered crowd in my head
Is going mild

This is the first place
In a long list of places
That I do not wish to be
I would answer all your questions
Were they not accusations
The one-way glass
Is making me nervous
Perhaps we should agree
To meet somewhere in the middle
And decide you were right all along

Soooo…

Roll up! Roll up!
Your cigarettes
And straightjacket superman sleeves
You'll need something to smoke
Between the scenes
While you're playing the debonair hero
Saving all those lonely, broken people
From their vices
And from themselves
One fucker at a time

Wake Me When It's Over

It's a candy floss snuff film
With a midnight screening at Disneyland
The blood-red carpet, wet
Trampled by famous monsters
The movie, universally lauded
Lives slaughtered
Starring all of our favourite religious deities
Without naming names

Hyper reality tears the truth asunder
Arousing our sense that we are informed
By the truth of eternal, cruel, horrific wars
That have no ending or beginning
No reasonable meaning
Yet they kill, maim and torture
Innocent people, indiscriminately

The good guys are the bad guys are the good guys are the…
It's never that simple but…
Fuck this
It's too much for me
There is no discernible difference
Between the propaganda and the reality
There is only vicarious
Sadistic
Voyeurism

I think I'll close the blinds
Turn out the lights
Lingering behind my eyes
Watch a horror movie or two
Bleed all over the microwave popcorn
And contemplate life as Art

The Trouble with Hair

Sleep
That mad slaver of luminescent darkness
Filled to the edges with concrete dreaming
Smear my eyelids in wet cement
And let me sleep

I want to bathe in the blood of my enemies
If you'll just point them out to me
To slice open their onion cerebrums
Like jubilant sparkling mirror balls
And dance in the disco blood
But I'd rather sleep
Yes
For the saving of lives
For fucks sake
And the sake of wet mattresses
Saturated with holy water and urine
Thrown off bridge impasses
Into oncoming, bladder bursting automobiles
Let me sleep

I am a bobbing
Of blobbing hair
A buffet of bouffant
Everything beneath me has been rendered invisible
Thank you I mutter
To everyone in particular

Wild-eyed, hello kissing women
Bury their immaculately chiselled faces into my locks
Are they searching for a key?
A needle stack sniff
Of smoke, nicotine gum fragments
And dandruff parmesan

I am better than this
When I am asleep
My hair is just better than me
Full stop

I want to smother the world in my hair
I want to suffocate Gaia
Via hair straighteners
And expensive, useless product
In strangulation's hands
Lubed onto the palms of the balding
Like gel, moose and petroleum jelly
Light me up
Rub your hands together with glee
I will be your happily ever after
Bon fire
Bobbing aflame
Between stretched to snapping party faces
Illuminating the eyes of disbelievers
Dangling from the end of sticks
Like pretty pink marshmallows
Melting albino pupils

Dying to be devoured by royalty
Snorted by the beautiful nostrils
Of bonny lasses
Like laundry powder cocaine
And the tortured, bleeding lashes
Of nine-tailed whips
And bad luck black cats
Buried in my hair

Oh, let me sleep
If not for the stopping of the death toll
Then for my own peace
At least
Let me sleep forever here

The Unimportance of Being Earnest (Hemingway)

Please do not unplug me from the wall
Please do not turn me off
Please do not attempt to reboot me
I will not work again
Please kill me with your kindness
For I have a snarky suspicion
That I do deserve to die

Please find it in your heart to forgive me
For I cannot forgive myself
Please look down upon me
Like the leper that I am
Searching for phantom limbs
On lost and dumfounded street corners
In an insomniac's sleeping quarters
On a deserted island
Populated by everything-in-vain

I offer my happy-meal hell to you
I offer you my severed spine and pickled mind
I offer you a gift of flatulent air
In an empty box

Please do not take my dreams away
For without them I cannot breathe
Please step away from the exit
For without your consent, I cannot leave
Please pretend that you care
For without your love, I do not exist

And to wonder…
I bled over all of this for me

All so that I could heal
All so that I could contrive another story
That didn't paint me
Like the word cannibal I am
So that I could suffer loudly, proudly
And without fear of reprisal
But dreams such as these
They rarely go according to plan

I want so badly to absorb your pain
I want to steal your nervous, shaking hands
I want to rewrap and re-gift them
To maddened statues and motionless strangers
To those who would give anything
For the chance to dance again

Please do not cut my cords
I am a lifeless box without them
Please do not tear out my tongue with your teeth
I only mean to kiss you in darkness
Somewhere cold and safe, secret and alone
Where I merely long to belong

I am remiss to exist
For to love all that is laid out
To abolish me
To negate me
To infiltrate the stronghold
That the damned built just for me
Is merely the folly
Of a poetic provocateur
This ill-starred, still scarred fool

If I was Wilde
I'd live in the Burroughs
If I was gay
I'd still be sad
So, draw the curtains pencil thin
Fill my open casket with popularity pills
Let the celebrations begin

And to think…
I bled over all of this for you
I shrugged the very earth from Atlas's shoulders
As you looked the other way

The Most Interesting Person You Know

Lift your love up
Alive and reapplying
For restitution
Truth would be an offence
To your beauty
Something rare and untameable
Projecting a palate
Of unpalatable
Faith

Squint my eyes
To see what has always been there?
Nod my head
I can see what lies beneath

Shall we pretend?
For now
Forever
And for all times
That we are
Truly
Who we say we are?

What a pretty self-portrait
What a cheap shot
Of in congruent cubism
Did you paint that?

Beauty is the enemy of truth
It is transient
Because it is a lie
A rippling fiction of comparisons
In my own mind's eye

Everything wonderful
Everything consumable
Is a regurgitation
Sexuality is vomit
Love is a disease
Ugliness and abomination
Are the only truths
Worth dying for

HEADLINE!
But I would say that
Wouldn't eye?

That is me
In your rear-view mirror
This is me
Waving handi-cupped
As you drive away

Yes, I am dead
Yes, you are alive
(Yawn)

Cumbersome dichotomies
Roar through red streetlights and stop signs
We ignore them
We rush
Like buttered knives through the pain

And you wonder why I am still smiling?

Hollowed torsos
Borne from Holy Wood endings
Suck in the pungent air
Of raw and tainted
Pop culture lungs
And
I
Am
Out
Of
Fucking
Excuses

Unreality is beauty is truth is paralytic misanthropy
Can I
Perchance
Munch on your crayons?

I'm drunk enough
I'm medicated enough
To spare us both the bother
Of friendship

Note to self:
Binary oppositions aren't particularly clever

The point of the game
Is to keep playing
Even when you know
You have lost
Hold back the tears
Roll the dice
And nod, yep
Just keep on nodding

Being dead is my talent
Yours is being interesting
The most interesting person you know

The Flavour of That Time of the Month

I refuse to censor myself
Imagine
The flyblown carcass of an eviscerated dog
Strewn across a gravel road
If I compromise
That will be me

I refuse to pander to trends
And attempt to delight shallow socialites
There is no 'scene' without scenesters
And I'm fading from their narcissistic radar
Like an irritating rash on the groin of a martyr
A rogue blip, on a perverse-onality trip

Imagine
A redneck in a pimped-out ute
Driving off into the sunset
A hit and run meth head
With blood-red, mongrel-stained headlights
And bullet holes for eyes
Given half a chance
He'd mow me down
In a split mind second
But I'd still get back up again

I'm the tenacious wart on a numb conscience
No matter how many times I'm cut out
I will return to haunt you
I will not go away

Imagine
I'm coming to a town like yours
I'll be riding up your spine
And pissing fiction
As if each link of your tarmacadam vertebrae
Were merely another bend in the road
Another downward step
On a spiral stairway to hell

So be yourself
And I will be me
If you're offended
Own it
Then get the fuck out of my way

The Way Out

Candid glamour
Costing you eternity
The way out is near
When you pay with your blood
Will the pain
The world
The constant bickering rain
Finally disappear?

Madness is in the holy water
You're swallowing truth
Making a timely spectacle
Third eye
Blue testicle
Time to examine the proof

The parade is winding
But the streets are straight
Such sadness in your heart
Where do you go?
When the line crosses you?
How do you correct death?
There are too many martyrs
And not enough laughter
To trade your brilliance
For your breath

Anti-hero Quest

1.

Ginger Ninja rolls the dice
Lawful evil with a heart of gold
He nonetheless has his charms
He shoots a nervous, sweaty glance
at the clock on his phone
There's nothing better to do to pass the time
The delivery is imminent

A painted miniature of a man
with gleaming pate and bulbous buddha belly
Ginger Ninja rides out the hours, minutes, seconds
and rolls still more dice
As time, like an agonisingly excited
Salvador Dali timepiece
Melts away

Should I leave my friend like this?
Should Ginger Ninja be left to his own devices?
An important, nay, life altering delivery
Hero Quest: the greatest board game in the multiverse
Is on its way to my door

The short answer is simple:
To Ragnarok with the repercussions!

Without so much as a perilous whimper
Armed with a bucket of imitation blood
and an imaginary broad sword
I step outside into the world that only exists
When I open the door

2.

When I return the flat is eerily quiet
Ginger Ninja is passed out on the lounge room floor
He is covered in unpainted miniatures,
Maps, modules, and memorandums scatter the room
A small trickle of drool descends
from the corner of his open mouth
His eyes are white quivering slits,
All colour has retreated, fleeing the scene
Rolling like departing thunder,
into the back of his head

A sheen of sweat beads on his pudgy, naked torso
Catching improbable light from a prying bulb
One hand has disappeared inside his shorts
the other circles a hairy, pert nipple

Aghast, I wipe at the protoplasmic ooze
That wells in my eyes
Like tear duct goob glue
'Hero Quest, what have you done to my friend?'

I nudge his inert, pasty ribcage with my boot
He snorts, burps, wheezes, and absently mumbles to himself
Girly giggling, as if bemused,
in some alien tongue
Then he rolls over onto his side
But there is no friendly ocean to shove him back into
There is no way to Free Willy

Is it all over for Ginger Ninja? I sadly muse

But then his eyes suddenly flicker open
Revealing two dilated, determined pupils
Fixated on purpose, and an undetermined,
Unknowable army of plastic Orcs
And perhaps even a fire breathing dragon
That only he can see

A studied air of calm enfolds him
He wipes the drool from his jowls and tastes it
Placing a salty fingertip to his tongue and smiling wickedly:
The sweet nectar of destiny

I snatch up each die and place them in his clammy palm
His fingers close over the six-sided bones,
cradling them, one at a time, with unyielding purpose

In protest of love and the Game itself:
Ginger Ninja rolls the dice.

A Place Where Nothingness is No Longer a Word

Reality is just another cage
No ins
No outs
Just smoke and fragments of glass
Mirrors in other people's feet
Red footprints in self-conscious hallways

Garrotte me with razor wire
But please, do it with a kind smile
Set my retinas alight
With someone else's box of wet matches
I can't see a damn thing
The way out
The way in
A locked and bolted door
Where my heart used to be
My chest is hollower than my head

I say a prayer at night
Just in case someone is listening
Please take me while I am sleeping
I care not for cotton-mouthed purgatories
Or the stories they tell
I just want it all to stop
Peacefully
With lithe yet ugly grace
An end to the dream
A full stop without pain

No unnecessary punctuation
No exclamation marked suicide
No coma
No comma
No bullshit

Death is a charming companion
Please, Your Highness
Take me out on the town
Take me dancing
Your Honour!
Your Horror!
Take me to a place where nothingness is no longer a word

Take my breath away

For Angels There to See

When the sky suffocates
In the darkness, pitch black,
When you thought it would be blue
I will be that thought never reached
A POINT without place
The laughter that shrouds
Your funerals in my ink
Sweating tepid tears
And streaking cheeks
With on-tab acid
And unholy bleach

Run
Run
The beetle in your brain
Trained to run
Through the traps
In the sky
From the voices inside
From Always
And Her blackened wings
You will run

Be warned
For I will surely catch you
Break into your shattered shell
Crack you open
Drink you
I shall
For Angels there to see

A cold white light
Shall penetrate your hiding place
Offering you nothing
But a gift of air
In an empty box
It is then
I shall descend
Splitting hairs within hairs
To clog your ears
Blind those pretty blue eyes
Of truant vision
And as you spill into the void
These fingers
Will write stories in your blood
For you alone
I will
For Angels there to see

Crawl inside your faith
An insect
Burrowing under milk-white skin
Laugh for you
Love for you
Steal your shaking hands
I shall
Hold you when you cry
Speak through your pain
Carve a lonely poetry
Into your head
For Angels there to see

It is the least I can do
For me
For you
Reach inside your chest
Tear the certainty from truth
Watch you grow
Festering, slow
Lap up your sickness
Drink gently of Divinity
As She drizzles from your lips

I shall
Devour you
For
I am you
Who else is there to be?

Rising, a damned horizon
Above your windowsill
Wearing a curtain smile
Parting the way
Paling before your love
In a marsh of dead tears

It is finally over…
Run
Run
The war in you
Is now undone

I cannot decide
I cannot choose
Between your eyes
Both screaming and murderous
Traitors of bickering,
Magnetic upstarts, those parts
That will never align
That will never repel
That will never know THIS again
Two learned pupils of the Worm
Neither willing
Nor bothered
To look upon this:
Sunken.
Defeated.
Invisible.
Face.

Love outwitted.

Masks

Labyrinths are built to cage clowns
They were designed by you and me

Masks are worn over masks are worn over masks

Wandering through the machine
with blinkers on
Asphyxiating on alone time
like a brown paper bag over a covid head
with bullet holes where eyes once danced
Counting down the daze
on a fingerless hand that may as well be a fist
On a leaking boat set adrift
like a plastic bag meandering
in a bottomless ocean of good intentions

Masks are worn over masks are worn over masks

Prank calls and empirical pasta
Rank cologne and far Q sneezes
Prayer beads and crucifixes
Wearing holy rubbers
It's all part of the scheduled entertainment vacuum
Drooling over you from afar
like Nosferatu's tampon
Pouring over you from the bar
like reprehensible vodka

Tear-shaped Swastika

Repeat after me
I am the canned laughter track
A last-minute replacement
For the live audience
With fond reminiscence
And a tear-shaped swastika
Caught in my eye
Do they have it…infamy?

Repeat after me
Echo my displacement
I dare you to press pause
Without leaving the harm chair
The breakdown
Has been televised
This sitcom is the dominion
Of distant, throbbing pincushions
Bleeding hearts bursting
From ribcage frights
Hitting
The shitting fans
The blood splatters
Projected on the walls
Of a hell caught in the spotlight
On a fourth-dimensional TV

Repeat after me
Mimic the symptoms of my disease
If you can stand the humiliation
There is a rung
Of this ludicrous ladder
You can skip
Entirely

The break-up song
Is on high rotation
On liquefied radio frequencies
My soul is an electrical socket
Penetrated
By a three-pronged power docket
And love is the enemy

Is there something other than despair?
That we can contribute to the mess?
How much loss
Can one toss into the wishing well?
These coins…
They have already been coined
These loins
Are parched with thirst
Sandpaper throats
Wrestle with wooden goats
In someone else's version
Of sexuality

Repeat after me
Program my disinformation
There is a list
Of blacked-out memories
Calendars pissed
On sober notoriety
The footage of us dancing
Has been wiped
From the dirty windscreens
Of eternity

Repeat after me
Or say nothing
I could care less
My flaws are covered
In the menstrual blood
Of muzzled wolves
And toothless fairies

Just keep moping
And mopping
There may be no stopping
The death toll
But we have plenty of photos
Of the corpses of heroes
And I am completely
And utterly
Over and Under the moon

The Severing of Strings

Are we just puppets?
Obsessed, reaching out
For the right to bear
Our own arms, for scissors
That would sever all these strings?
Would we fall limp
Into some fictional hellfire
At whatever God strikes our fancies
Smouldering feet?

A God that would –
Once freed from our torture
And grim, truthless faith
And two-way mirror love-ins
At cheap hotels
When anyone could be watching
With stealable towels
And chained-down Bibles
On the edge of forever
– *Explain us to ourselves*

We see things
As we see ourselves
We live a lifetime of lies
Just to fit in
We don't need these Gods
Any more than they need us
Are we not inundated, corrupted by fickle desires?
And prayers, so poisonous
They inform the flow of take all you can,
And then run like buggery.

Are we not entertained?
'Thou shall not think'
Is this the final commandment?
'Love thy neighbour
But choose your suburb carefully'*
And on and on and on…

Will we get a prize for choosing correctly?
At some point will we win?
Something
Anything
For fucks sake
To make this excruciating carousel,
And the game show host
With the game show teeth
Worth sparing
Or should we knock his molars right out of his head?
And spray the front row droolers
Those that laugh on cue
Applaud on cue
Vomit on cue
With real, authenticated
Empty game show gums
And lashings of blood,
Pissing like a fountain
Like golden-filled teeth, missing
His body still quivering,
Still in an expensive
Made for television suit
His neck, now an oozing stump

The bells of bullshit
Hear them ring out
Long after the apocalypse has played itself out
Like the panned flutes of the piper
Smashed repeatedly
Over our pre-hollowed, wooden
Explosion timed to perfection, heads

Let the ticking of the bombs continue
Let the tocks and the clocks
Keep us alive
Empty-brained, entertained
Until the end of time as we know it
Or at least until the next
Sponsored by the monster
Commercial break

The Imaginary Play

What is this monster?
Caught in cut throats
Like a lump of tangled twine
I am at a loss to win
The indescribable knots
Tied up by the tyrannical testimonies
Of the tried and the tested, yet failing
Moods of carnivorous vine
Filling my every silence
With yet more hollow words

The mouth blabbering
Like a sphincterous cavity
Caught on the end of a stick
It is incoherent and pointed
At the lent ears, melting
In the pit of hell's fire
Examining everything
As if there were some truth in sanity

So, unlearn the information
Reprogram the mind
Slaver over
The digitally wired tongues
Lashing at logic, in this land
Of sitting right next to nothing

One wonders
If there is reason enough to go on
Statues of statutes
Are built up
Then torn down
Laws and constitutions
Are rewritten to rewrite
Personal histories
Taking the sense of self, itself
Away from us

I would rather wither
In sanctimonious woe
Than vomit on pages
Already torn and stinking
Of regurgitated love
And repetitions
Of parrot and carrot chunked
Passion plays
That leave me alone
To wonder
Why the curtains parted
To reveal an empty stage
And an actor-less
Directionless
Shaking-spear matinee

The tragedy
Is that there was never a play to begin with
And I am just another throbbing member
Of an invisible audience
Sitting among imaginary critics
That have been robbed of all dignity
And left to sit in silence
Staring into a theatre of absurd
Nonsensical
Emptiness
That will no doubt get rave reviews
For being cutting edge
And really saying something
By saying nothing
Absolutely fucking nothing at all
Nonetheless

But then I wonder
Hang on…
Didn't I write that play?
Am I not the star of that show?
And then I realise the obvious
And I feel like a goddamn idiot
A meaningless twit
A non-event
Just like my imaginary play
In a mediocre poem
In a word
Futile

Yet in some dark
Fucked-up place
In my deluded mind
I wait, still
For the glowing reviews
To arrive, flowing freely
Like the cheap red plonk
At the castless after-party
Flooding the neural pathways
Of a pickled, but tickled pink
Storm water brain

Upon Reflection

'Oh, enough about ME!' he said.
'Enough!'
Waving his hands over my ears
As if they were burning
And he was merely fanning the flames
Of naïve indifference

'Enough, enough about ME!'
He declared
And his nostrils flared
Like pupils dilating in portaloo twilight
Absorbing all life
Flushing the evidence away
As profound as a conversation
Between long-dead satellites
Orbiting a barren planet

It was all just second-hand smoke
And one-way mirrors
Decorating the perforated walls
Of the lungs we secretly shared

'What do YOU think of me?' he asked.
And at last
I laughed at the log in his eye
As it barrelled like bone marrow
Down his cheek
Into a piss stain of skeleton tears

So, I slammed a gavel down
On the mirror
Shattering the magic
For everyone and no one in particular
I lit a wet cigarette
Scratched at my retreating balls
And marvelled at the wonder of it all

Fat from Dreams

They read me my writes
They tattooed the safety instructions
Upon my furrowed brow
Now
The jackhammering of the needle
And the point of the ink
The swirling of water
Down the drainpipe kink
Can never be flushed away

The trolling of the church bell
Awoke in me the urge
To scale the castle walls
I swung from the parapets
With a lithe and fantastic tongue
The taste of the skin was bitter
The whip's bite was sweet
As chariot

A thousand angry wasps
Stung me back to sleep
I ate the astral pain
An obese release
And now
I am fat from dreams

Still, what the oracle tells me
Could be real
Rubbish is tangible
And in the tip of the garbage flat
The brim of a mad hat
Is now my noose

And I am slipping

Darling, don't leave me dangling
Sweetness, don't leave me in distress
I could care less
For the company of silhouettes
I yearn for some healing
To keep the leaking boats at bay

Would you forgive me?
If I were guilty
Would you release my soul?
On cassette
Would you wretch upon my recordings?
Real to reel
Or am I allowed to forget?

The night is short
I am bathed in a cruel digital glow
And I know
As long as those eyes are watching me
I will never be alone

Voices

(For Andy)

As long as he could not remember
The fiend had always been there
An implant, brooding
Waiting in the shadows of youth
Activated by a strange dawning
A myriad of pointed jibes, now manifest
Buried deep within his brain

It spoke at him constantly
Rattling off insults and taunts
Not a minute went by
Without a cruel dig or a dull, perilous whisper
Always at the expense
Of his frail sense
That what was deep inside of him
Was outside of him as well

When the fiend was silent
The voices were supplanted
By the incessant tick-tock
Of a snarling mind clock
Jackknifing the space behind his eyes
Counting down
To an explosion that promised freedom
A chance to mutate in the darkness
To the luscious strings of an orchestra
To the lurid music
Of irreconcilable peace

A cacophony of snarling hounds
Straining at their leashes, hell bound
The gnashing of tombstone teeth
Always beneath
Breaking away, creating a new, tangible
Terrifying reality

If only Jesus was a ghostly carpenter
Sent to visit him in the never after
A holy man, to man the drill
To burrow deep into his cranium
Retrieve the buried implant
Unearth the cackling fiend
Parade it before the Changelings
And the Seraphim
To show them
That the Demon's final deal
Is all too real

Yet trephination
Requires determined drilling
Purgatory, by its very nature
Keeps the kindest hearts
Right where they are
Until an unearthly hell decides to take them
Until all of heaven is disproven

The murderer of minds, invisible
The de-sadist, exploiting all secrets
Paying for thought crimes
With death pennies
Wet from the blood of martyrs

Thoughts, fragile and so human
So proud, feet of clay
Plodding through the doldrums of ordinary mud
In a suit of unsuitable armour
Captured by the secret war
Humiliated, by cruel and laughing eyes

A study of serpents and soul-caged ink
Of torment, clipped wings and courage
Of another canvas, yearning
To be filled with untold wonder
Paint pen strokes
Configurations of rogue colour
Churning in the deepest wishing well
Banished from foul subservience
To the multitude of voices
To the taunting, within and without
Never to be silent
Never to be free

He is propelled onward
Rolling like demented thunder
Raging through fields of dark imagining
Killing us all
With fiery carved lines
Lashings of splendour and smoke
Unleashed, like the flood
Of a wounded wolf's blood

Defiant
He creates more magic
than is permissible
With the lightning tip
Of his enchanted pen

www.ingramcontent.com/pod-product-compliance
Lightning Source LLC
Chambersburg PA
CBHW050259120526
44590CB00016B/2410